SOUND

By

Steffi Cavell-Clarke

©2016
Book Life
King's Lynn
Norfolk PE30 4LS

ISBN: 978-1-78637-107-2

Written by:
Steffi Cavell-Clarke

Edited by:
Grace Jones

Designed by:
Danielle Jones

PHOTO CREDITS

Abbreviations: l-left, r-right, b-bottom,
t-top, c-centre, m-middle.

Front cover – Luis Molinero. 2 – Sergey Novikov. 4 – Brian A Jackson. 5– Tom
Wang. 6 – Ninell. 7 – Luis Molinero. 8 – Asier Romero . In Green. 10 – an-
dras_csontos. 11l – Lim Yong Hian, 11r – Utekhina Anna. 12 – Asier Romero.
13l – Sonsedska Yuliia, 13r – Eric Isselee. 14 – Beneda Miroslav. 15 – rarach.
16 – Szasz-Fabian Jozsef. 17 – maxim ibragimov. 18 – Early Spring.
19 – Eric Isselee. 20 – Valua Vitaly. 21 – Andrey_Popov. 23 – Tan Kian Khoon.
Images are courtesy of Shutterstock.com.
With thanks to Getty Images, Thinkstock Photo and iStockphoto.

CONTENTS

Words that look like **this** can be found in the glossary on page 24.

What is SCIENCE?

Where do sounds come from?

How do we hear sounds from far away?

Can we see or touch sounds?

Science can answer many difficult questions we may have and help us to understand the world around us.

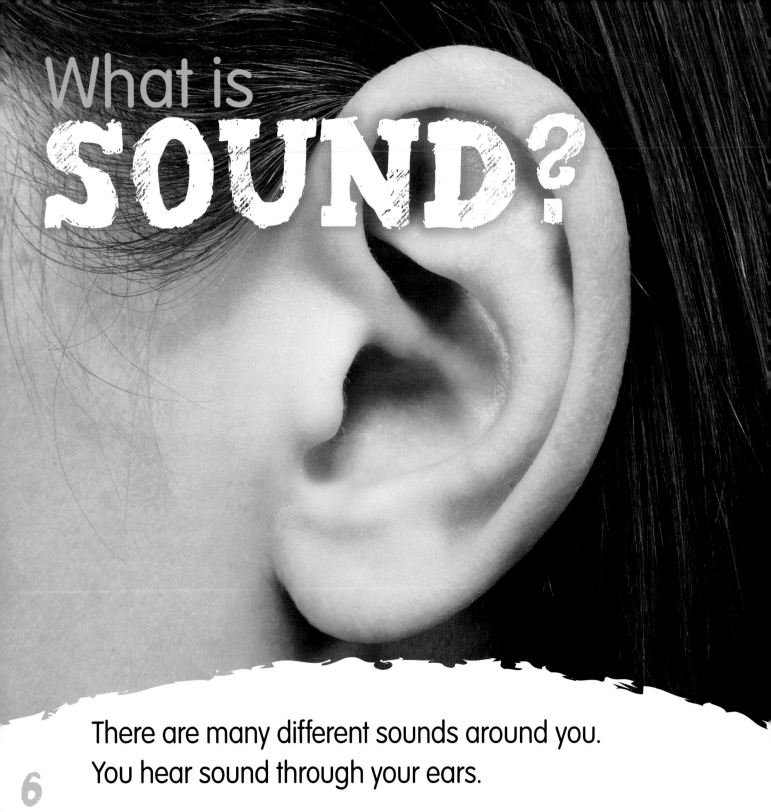

What is SOUND?

There are many different sounds around you.
You hear sound through your ears.

6

Sounds can be quiet, loud, high or low. Listen carefully to the sounds around you. What can you hear?

Where Does SOUND Come From?

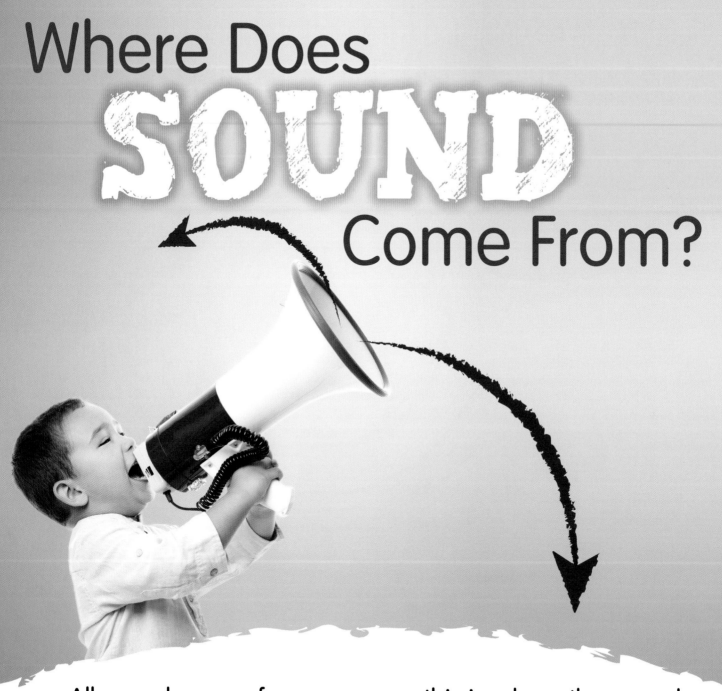

All sounds come from a **source**, this is where the sound starts. There are many different sources of sound.

Lots of things can make a sound. People, dogs, cars and televisions can all be sources of sound.

9

How Do We  HEAR?

You use your **sense** of hearing to listen to sound.
Sound **vibrations** travel through the air to your ears.

The insides of your ears send a message to your brain.
Your brain tells you what sound you are hearing.

Meeow

Making SOUNDS

People can make sound by talking, shouting or singing. You can use the sounds made by your voice to speak to other people.

Animals also make sounds. Different types of animal make different sounds.

What sound does
a cat make?

What sound does
a dog make?

Loud
SOUNDS

A sound is loud when the sound vibrations
are bigger and travel further through the air.

You can hear louder sounds from further away than quieter sounds.

You can hear loud thunder from the sky.

Quiet SOUNDS

A sound is quieter when the sound vibrations are smaller.

You can make a quiet sound by whispering. What other quiet sounds can you make?

High and Low
SOUNDS

Sounds can be high or low. The difference is called pitch. When you blow a whistle, it makes a high-pitched sound.

Lots of sounds have a low pitch. This makes the sound vibrations move more slowly through the air.

A lion's roar makes a low-pitched sound.

Musical SOUNDS

You can use musical **instruments** to make many different sounds. A guitar has strings on it which are plucked to make different sounds.

Super SENSES

A person who is **blind** can use different sounds to help them to cross the road.

Let's EXPERIMENT!

Do you know how sound moves? Let's find out!

YOU WILL NEED:

2 plastic cups
Sharp pencil
Piece of string
(about 1 metre long)

STEP 1

Ask an adult to carefully pierce a small hole in the bottom of each cup using a sharp pencil.

STEP 2

Thread one end of the string through each hole and tie a knot at each end.

STEP 3

Give a friend a cup and stretch out the string. Let your friend hold the cup to their ear as you talk into the other end.

TOP TIP:
Ask an adult to help you!

RESULTS:

The sound vibrations from your voice move along the string into the other cup. This will allow your friend to hear the sounds coming from your voice.

23

GLOSSARY

blind	cannot see
instruments	things that can make musical sounds
sense	something that helps you to see, smell, touch, taste or hear the things around you
source	where something comes from
vibrations	shaking movements

INDEX